WITHDRAWN

Great Explorers

Neil Armstrong

by Jim Olhoff

Visit us at
www.abdopublishing.com

Published by ABDO Publishing Company, PO Box 398166, Minneapolis, MN 55439.
Copyright ©2014 by Abdo Consulting Group, Inc. International copyrights reserved in all countries. No part of this book may be reproduced in any form without written permission from the publisher. ABDO & Daughters™ is a trademark and logo of ABDO Publishing Company.

Printed in the United States of America, North Mankato, Minnesota
052013
092013

 PRINTED ON RECYCLED PAPER

Editor: John Hamilton
Graphic Design: Sue Hamilton
Cover Design: Neil Klinepier
Cover Photo: NASA
Interior Photos & Illustrations: All images NASA except: AP-pg 24; Courtesy of the estate of Neil Armstrong-pg 10; iStockphoto-compass illustration; Thinkstock-grunge map background illustration.

ABDO Booklinks

To learn more about Great Explorers, visit ABDO Publishing Company online. Web sites about Great Explorers are featured on our Book Links pages. These links are routinely monitored and updated to provide the most current information available. Web site: www.abdopublishing.com

Library of Congress Control Number: 2013931673

Cataloging-in-Publication Data

Ollhoff, Jim.
 Neil Armstrong / Jim Ollhoff.
  p. cm. -- (Great explorers)
ISBN 978-1-61783-963-4
1. Armstrong, Neil, 1932-2012--Juvenile literature. 2. Astronauts--United States--Biography--Juvenile literature. 3. Project Apollo (U.S.)--Juvenile literature. 4. Space flight to the moon--Juvenile literature. I. Title.
629.45/0092--dc23
[B]   2013931673

Contents

The Space Race

Below: The Moon photographed from Apollo 11 in July 1969.

Since before civilization began, human beings have been staring up at the Moon. They wondered why it was so bright, why it traveled across the sky, and where it came from. Throughout history, people looked at it, studied it, wrote stories about it, and photographed it. But on July 20, 1969, American astronaut Neil Alden Armstrong became the first human being to actually walk on the surface of the Moon.

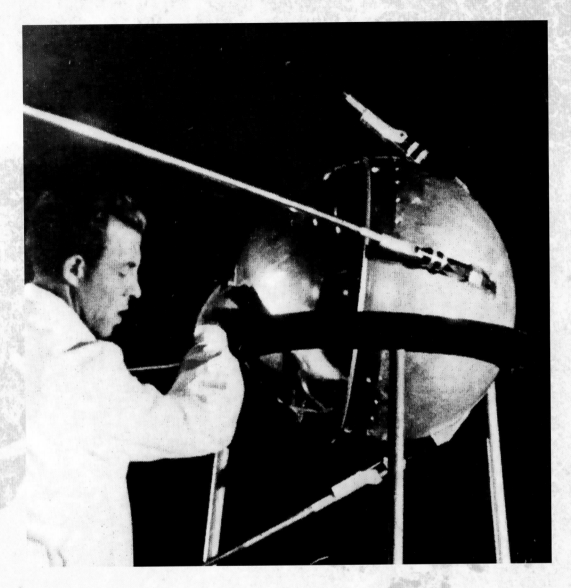

The Moon-landing story started in 1957. During the 1950s, there were two big superpowers in the world: the United States and the Soviet Union. The Soviet Union included Russia and a collection of neighboring territories. The two superpowers were in a Cold War—tensions were high, but there were no military battles between the two countries. However, the United States and the Soviet Union were always suspicious of each other.

Above: On October 4, 1957, the Soviet Union successfully launched *Sputnik 1*. The small unmanned space satellite transmitted a radio signal for 22 days.

Above: The Soviet Union placed the first man in space on April 12, 1961. The next month, President John F. Kennedy spoke to the United States Congress. Kennedy emphasized that the United States needed to catch up and overtake the Soviet Union in the race to control space.

On October 4, 1957, the Soviet Union launched a small unmanned space satellite called *Sputnik 1.* It transmitted radio signals for 22 days. Then, after about three months in orbit, it fell back toward Earth and burned up in the atmosphere. Leaders in the United States were caught off guard. They suddenly feared that the United States would be left behind in science, engineering, and space exploration. People called for immediate advances in the space program. School curriculums across the country changed to include more math and science.

Leaders in the United States rushed their rocket program forward. On December 6, 1957, the country was ready to launch an unmanned Vanguard rocket. However, it exploded on the launch pad.

On April 12, 1961, Soviet cosmonaut Yuri Gagarin became the first human being in space. This reinforced American fears about falling behind.

Above: Neil Armstrong sits inside the Lunar Module as it rests on the lunar surface after completion of his historic moonwalk. As he stepped onto the Moon, Armstrong said, "That's one small step for a man. One giant leap for mankind."

On May 25, 1961, President John F. Kennedy spoke to the United States Congress. He said, "I believe that this nation should commit itself to achieving the goal, before this decade is out, of landing a man on the Moon and returning him safely to Earth."

With these words, the Apollo program was born. And on July 20, 1969, American Neil Armstrong became the first man to walk on the Moon.

Neil Armstrong: Early Years

Opposite Page: An early portrait of Neil Armstrong. Armstrong enlisted in the United States Navy in 1947. He trained as a military pilot, and at age 20 became the youngest pilot in his squadron.

Neil Alden Armstrong was born on his grandparents's farm near the small town of Wapakoneta, Ohio, on August 5, 1930. His father was an auditor for the state of Ohio, so the family had to move frequently. They eventually settled back in Wapakoneta.

Armstrong was interested in flying as a young boy. He built model airplanes and read books about flying. He worked many jobs to earn money so he could take flying lessons. He earned his student pilot's license even before he had his driver's license.

Armstrong graduated from high school in 1947. He enlisted in the United States Navy, which gave him a college scholarship in return for later service. Armstrong went to Purdue University in Indiana and majored in aeronautical engineering.

Before Armstrong could complete his college degree, the Navy called him into active duty. He reported to Pensacola Naval Air Station in Florida in 1949. He trained as a military pilot, and at age 20 became the youngest pilot in his squadron.

Neil Armstrong's Early Career

I n the early 1950s, the United States was involved in the Korean War (1950-1953). The United States supported South Korea in its war against North Korea. Many United States soldiers were sent to fight.

The Navy sent Ensign Neil Armstrong to South Korea in 1951, stationed aboard the aircraft carrier USS *Essex*. He flew 78 combat missions and earned an Air Medal with two Gold Stars, the Korean Service Medal, and an Engagement Star.

On September 3, 1951, he had to parachute out of a damaged airplane after being hit by gunfire.

Armstrong left the Navy in 1952 and returned to the United States. In 1955, he finished his degree in aeronautical engineering at Indiana's Purdue University. (In 1970 he earned a masters degree in aerospace engineering from the University of Southern California in Los Angeles, California.)

Below: Neil Armstrong married Janet Shearon in 1956.

Neil Armstrong was a test pilot for the X-15 high-speed rocket plane at the Dryden Flight Research Center in 1960.

After earning his college degree, Armstrong joined a government agency called the National Advisory Committee for Aeronautics. He worked as an engineer, test pilot, and administrator. In 1958, that organization became NASA, the National Aeronautics and Space Administration.

As a test pilot, Armstrong flew more than 200 different kinds of aircraft, including jets, rockets, and gliders. He also flew the North American X-15, a famous experimental high-speed rocket plane that could travel more than 4,500 miles per hour (7,242 kph).

Neil Armstrong married Janet Shearon in 1956. Their son Eric was born in 1957. Their daughter Karen was born in 1959, but tragically died of a brain tumor three years later. In 1962, their third child, Mark, was born.

Command Pilot of Gemini 8

Gemini 8 launched on March 16, 1966.

In 1962, Armstrong was accepted into NASA's astronaut program. NASA's Gemini space program was a series of 12 missions between 1964 and 1966. Most of them were manned missions that sent people into space. The mission goals included testing equipment and procedures. The missions also prepared many of the astronauts who would eventually fly to the Moon in the Apollo missions.

Armstrong was selected to be the command pilot for Gemini 8. This was the 12th manned space flight for the United States, and Armstrong's first. Gemini 8 launched on March 16, 1966. Armstrong and one other astronaut, David Scott, were sent up in space for a series of maneuvers and procedures. One of the flight tasks was to dock two different vehicles together, which had never been done before. Armstrong successfully docked his own spaceship to an unmanned spaceship.

Astronauts Neil Armstrong (left) and David Scott train to command Gemini 8 in 1966.

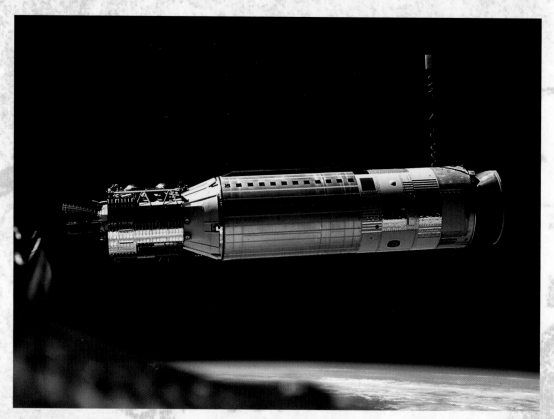

Above: Gemini 8 rendezvous with the unmanned Agena vehicle in orbit over Earth.

Shortly after the two ships docked, they started to spin uncontrollably. A malfunction was causing one of the Gemini 8 thrusters to fire, causing the roll. Armstrong knew he had to disengage from the other ship. But when he did, it made the spinning worse. The ship began to spin about one revolution every second. Gemini 8 was spinning so fast that it was difficult for the astronauts to move. They were in danger of losing consciousness. Further, the firing thruster was quickly exhausting their fuel. Armstrong remained composed and calm. He knew that the only way to save their lives was to scrub the rest of the mission and start the reentry process. Shortly after activating the reentry system, Armstrong had control of the spacecraft. They safely splashed down in the Pacific Ocean. Armstrong's quick thinking and expert piloting saved the astronauts.

Above: Astronauts Neil Armstrong and David Scott sit with their spacecraft hatches open while awaiting the arrival of the recovery ship, the USS *Leonard F. Mason,* after the completion of their Gemini 8 mission. They are assisted by military divers.

The Apollo Program

Below: The crew of Apollo 1, Virgil "Gus" Grissom, Ed White, and Roger Chaffee, were killed when a fire broke out while they were working in the spacecraft's cabin in 1967.

The Gemini program tested equipment and trained astronauts for the Apollo missions, which would land astronauts on the Moon. Each Apollo mission would build on previous missions, thoroughly testing equipment and procedures.

Apollo 1 was scheduled to launch on February 21, 1967. However, a terrible tragedy struck. On January 27, as the three astronauts were doing tests in the spacecraft's cabin, a fire erupted. Astronauts Virgil Grissom, Ed White, and Roger Chaffee died in the fire.

NASA cancelled all flights for the next 20 months until the problem could be investigated and corrected. When the Apollo flights resumed, NASA sent unmanned flights into space to test equipment, especially the rocket's ability to start and shut off at the correct times.

Apollo 7 was the first manned launch since the Apollo 1 disaster. Apollo 7, with three astronauts aboard, launched on October 11, 1968. It orbited the Earth for 11 days as the crew tested life-support equipment.

Apollo 8 launched on December 21, 1968. It left Earth's orbit, went to the Moon, and orbited the Moon 10 times without landing. It returned safely to Earth on December 27. Apollo 9 and Apollo 10 also orbited the Moon without landing, conducting tests that would prepare for the Apollo 11 Moon-landing mission.

Left: Apollo 8 launched on December 21, 1968. Astronauts Frank Borman, James Lovell, and William Anders traveled to the Moon and orbited it 10 times before returning safely to Earth.

Apollo 11

Years of preparation, training, and experimentation came together in 1969. It was time to actually land on the Moon and send astronauts out to walk on the lunar surface. Neil Armstrong was chosen to command the Apollo 11 mission. The crew also included astronauts Michael Collins and Edwin "Buzz" Aldrin. Apollo 11 was launched on July 16, 1969. It circled the Earth one-and-a-half times, and then headed for the Moon.

On July 19, Apollo 11 began orbiting the Moon. The main Apollo spacecraft was called the Command Module, and was named *Columbia.* It was docked with a separate Lunar Module, named *Eagle.* The plan was to have Armstrong and Aldrin land *Eagle* on the Moon while Collins piloted *Columbia* in orbit.

Above: The *Eagle* Lunar Module leaves Apollo 11's Command Module *Columbia* on the way to the Moon's surface. The Earth rises in the background.

On July 20, *Eagle* began its decent. The astronauts were aiming for a place on the Moon called the Sea of Tranquility, which was thought to be flat, with no rocky outcroppings. However, Armstrong and Aldrin realized they were off course. The spacecraft's computer was overshooting their original target, and was going to land in an area with dangerous boulders and uneven ground. Armstrong took manual control and landed *Eagle* in a safe place. Mission controllers back on Earth at NASA's Mission Control Center in Houston, Texas, held their breath as they waited for a radio signal from Armstrong. Finally, they heard him say, "Houston, Tranquility Base here. The *Eagle* has landed."

After a few hours on the Moon inside the Lunar Module, Armstrong opened the door and descended the stairs. With more than half a billion people on Earth watching the grainy images from the Moon on their TV set, Armstrong stepped onto the lunar surface. He uttered these now-famous words: "That's one small step for a man. One giant leap for mankind."

About 20 minutes later, Buzz Aldrin joined Armstrong on the lunar surface. They planted an American flag, and collected samples of soil and rocks. They took photographs and performed other experiments. Armstrong and Aldrin spent about two-and-a-half hours on the surface of the Moon, and then went back inside *Eagle*.

Astronaut Neil A. Armstrong, Mission Commander, works at the Lunar Module. The United States flag and a solar-wind composition experiment are visible.

A few hours later, the pair blasted off from the Moon's surface and then docked with the orbiting *Columbia* spacecraft. After Armstrong and Aldrin transferred to *Columbia*, the Lunar Module was jettisoned, and the astronauts began the journey back to Earth.

On July 24, 1969, *Columbia* splashed down in the Pacific Ocean, and was picked up by Navy vessels. NASA scientists didn't know if there were germs living on the lunar surface, so the three astronauts were forced to spend 21 days in isolation.

After their quarantine, the astronauts were given a hero's welcome. They were the stars of a New York City ticker-tape parade, and were given many awards.

The Apollo Program Continues

Below: The Apollo 13 Command Module is recovered. Against all odds, astronauts Jim Lovell, John Swigert and Fred Haise returned safely.

NASA launched Apollo 12 on November 14, 1969. Five days later, Apollo 12's Lunar Module landed on the Moon. This time, the astronauts spent more than a day on the lunar surface. The mission ended successfully with a splashdown back on Earth on November 24.

Apollo 13 blasted off on April 11, 1970. On their way to the Moon, an oxygen tank exploded. The craft was crippled, but they were far enough along in their mission that they continued to the Moon. They used the Moon's gravity to send them back to Earth. The crew had a shortage of power, oxygen, heat, and drinking water, but they persevered. With the help of dedicated NASA workers on Earth, the astronauts safely splashed down on April 17.

Apollo 17 Astronaut Harrison "Jack" Schmitt stands near the U.S. flag during NASA's final lunar landing mission in the Apollo series in 1972. The Lunar Module (LM) is at left and the Lunar Roving Vehicle (LRV) is in the background.

Apollo 14 and 15 went to the Moon in 1971. Apollo 16 and 17 landed in 1972. All four missions conducted a variety of experiments, and all returned home safely.

Several more Apollo Moon missions were scheduled, but they were cancelled due to budget cutbacks. An Apollo spacecraft was used on a mission in July 1975. It was a joint mission between the United States and the Soviet Union. The Apollo spacecraft and a Soviet Soyuz spacecraft docked in space. It marked the end of the space race that had started with the Soviet launch of *Sputnik 1* in 1957. The Apollo-Soyuz mission helped ease the long-running tension between the two countries.

Neil Armstrong: Later Years

Below: Neil Armstrong (front by shuttle model) served on the committee to investigate the 1986 space shuttle *Challenger* explosion (inset).

After returning from space, Armstrong became NASA's Deputy Associate Administrator for Aeronautics. In this position, he coordinated and managed research and technology. In 1971, he accepted a position at the University of Cincinnati to teach aerospace engineering. He taught there until 1979.

After his teaching job, he spent 10 years as the chairman of Computing Technologies for Aviation, a company based in Charlottesville, Virginia.

Challenger explosion.

Armstrong served on two investigation panels at NASA. The first was for the Apollo 13 incident. He served on the committee to probe what had happened and how to keep it from happening again. He also served on the committee to investigate the space shuttle *Challenger* explosion on January 28, 1986.

Above: On July 20, 2009, Neil Armstrong (tan suit), Buzz Aldrin (left) and Michael Collins (center) meet with President Barack Obama on the 40th anniversary of the Apollo 11 lunar landing.

While many famous people cash in on their celebrity status, Neil Armstrong lived a quiet and humble life. He declined most speaking engagements and most requests for interviews. He remained an advocate for sending astronauts into space, but mostly stayed out of the public spotlight.

In 2012, Armstrong had surgery for cardiovascular problems. He had complications from that surgery, and died on August 25, 2012. He was 82 years old.

Armstrong's Legacy

Opposite Page:
Neil Armstrong works on prelaunch activities prior to the liftoff of Gemini 8 on March 16, 1966. Below: An astronaut's footprint on the Moon's surface. Armstrong became the first person to walk on the Moon on July 20, 1969.

After Armstrong died, President Barack Obama said, "Neil was among the greatest of American heroes— not just of his time, but of all time." His Apollo 11 partner Buzz Aldrin said that Armstrong was a "true American hero and the best pilot I ever knew."

Neil Armstrong represented the biggest and best dreams of the day. To put someone on the Moon, and have him walk around on the lunar surface, was a fantastic achievement. There was a feeling that if people could do that, they could do anything. Any goal is possible with work, study, and ingenuity. Landing on the Moon was a landmark in human history.

Shortly after Armstrong's death, his family released this statement: "For those who may ask what they can do to honor Neil, we have a simple request. Honor his example of service, accomplishment, and modesty, and the next time you walk outside on a clear night and see the Moon smiling down at you, think of Neil Armstrong and give him a wink."

Timeline

1930, August 5 Neil Armstrong is born in Wapakoneta, Ohio.

1947 Neil Armstrong graduates from high school.

1949 Armstrong reports to Pensacola Naval Air Station in Florida.

1950-1953 The years of the Korean War. Armstrong flies 78 combat missions.

1955 Armstrong earns a bachelor's degree in aeronautical engineering from Purdue University in Indiana.

1956 Neil Armstrong marries Janet Shearon.

1957, October 4 The Soviet Union launches the *Sputnik I* satellite, igniting the space race.

1961, April 12 Soviet cosmonaut Yuri Gagarin becomes the first human being in space.

1966, March 16 Armstrong and David Scott fly Gemini 8. The flight almost ends in tragedy.

1969, July 16 Apollo 11 launches with Neil Armstrong as commander.

1969, July 20 Neil Armstrong and Buzz Aldrin fly the *Eagle* Lunar Module and land on the Moon. Neil Armstrong becomes the first man to walk on the surface of the Moon.

1969, July 24 Apollo 11 splashes down safely in the Pacific Ocean. The astronauts receive a hero's welcome.

Neil Armstrong puts on his helmet on July 16, 1969, the Apollo 11 launch day.

1971	Armstrong retires from NASA and becomes a college professor teaching aerospace engineering at the University of Cincinnati in Cincinnati, Ohio.
1982-1992	Armstrong works as chairman of Computing Technologies for Aviation in Charlottesville, Virginia.
2012, August 25	Neil Armstrong dies of complications from heart surgery.

Glossary

AERONAUTICS

The study of how things fly through the air.

APOLLO SPACE PROGRAM

An American space exploration program that ran from 1963 to 1972. Run by the National Aeronautics and Space Administration (NASA), the program's goal was to land astronauts on the Moon and return them safely to Earth. The first Moon landing was achieved by Apollo 11 on July 20, 1969.

ASTRONAUT

An American who flies in space.

COLD WAR

The Cold War was a time of political, economic, and cultural tension between the United States and its allies and the Soviet Union and other Communist nations. It lasted from about 1947, just after the end of World War II, until the early 1990s, when the Soviet Union collapsed and Communism was no longer a major threat to the United States.

COMMAND MODULE

The part of a spaceship in which the astronauts live, communicate with the control center on Earth, and operate the ship's controls.

COSMONAUT

A Russian astronaut.

EAGLE

The name of the lunar landing module on Apollo 11. On July 20, 1969, *Eagle* carried astronauts Neil Armstrong and Edwin "Buzz" Aldrin Jr. to the surface of the Moon.

MISSION CONTROL

The group of people on Earth who support the activities of astronauts during a manned space flight.

NATIONAL AERONAUTICS AND SPACE ADMINISTRATION (NASA)

A United States government agency started in 1958. NASA's goals include space exploration, as well as increasing people's understanding of Earth, our solar system, and the universe.

QUARANTINE

To place someone with a potentially deadly disease, germ, or infection, in a place where they cannot come in contact with any other non-infected person. In the 1960s, astronauts were placed in quarantine for several weeks to be sure they did not bring back any kind of unknown germ from space.

SPACE RACE

A competition between the Soviet Union and the United States in the 1950s, 1960s, and 1970s to be the first in various areas of space exploration. Some consider the Soviet Union's launch of the first artificial satellite (*Sputnik I*) on October 4, 1957, to be the start of the space race.

SPLASHDOWN

When some spacecraft return to Earth, they land in the ocean—thus, a splashdown.

SPUTNIK 1

The first space satellite, sent up by the Soviet Union on October 4, 1957, which many people believe ignited the space race.

TEST PILOT

A person who flies new or experimental aircraft to test the machine's flight worthiness.

Index